CROCHET BRALETTE PATTERNS

BEST CROCHET BRALETTES AND BRA CUP PATTERNS

LINDA BILLY

TABLE OF CONTENTS

INTRODUCTION

Modest crochet bralette may completely change the look of your summer wardrobe and also give you a better look during your outing.

Bralette, either worn alone, is far more fitting and suitable than wearing bra. You can wear a bralette under your clothing as a substitute to a bra, even at the beach or garden on hot days. Are you ready to try your hand to make your first crochet bralette? Here are some of our favorite crochet bralette patterns.

In this book, we will discuss step by step approach on how you can create a crochet bralette and we will also discuss various patterns you can create at home or during your free time.

PART 1: BASIC UNDERSTANDING OF CROCHET.

Before we get into crochet bralette it is essential we understand the basic things relating to crochet. This will be helpful for beginners who don't really have ideas on how to crochet and its process.

Many of us have come across crochet in one way or another. The fine loop-like structure and brilliant thread colors are a unique approach to spice up the pattern of everyday design. It is the act of generating textiles by interconnecting loops of yarn, thread, or utilizing a hook to interlock loop of yarn, thread or strand. The word "Crochet" comes from the French and it means "little hook."

COMPONENTS OF CROCHETING

A crochet hook can be used to create a crochet using materials like metal, wood, even plastic. It can be produced either commercially or even in artisan crafts. Crochet thread is composed of mercerized cotton that has a smaller diameter as well as a denser pile than ordinary yarn.

BRIEF HISTORY OF CROCHETING

In 1823, the term crochet was first used in the Dutch periodical Penélopé. The oldest English state of garments made of cloth that was formed by using a loop yarn with a hook. There are some pieces of evidence that French tambour needlework and crochet have a similar relationship. Diderot's Encyclopedia, published in 1763, detailed the previous manner of creation. Ivory, bone, even wooden hooks, as well as steel needles, have been referenced in several different works.

Crochet was first used in Ireland throughout the Great Irish Hunger (1845–1849) all the way through the 19th century as a method of famine relief. Crochet lace was a source of income for impoverished Irish peasants.

As a key component of the famine relief effort, crocheting was also taught in schools. The Irish migration brought the craft to the Americas. Irish crochet is said to have been invented by

Mademoiselle Riego de la Blanchardiere. In 1846, she released the first book of patterns. Irish lace gained popularity in Europe and America, and it was mass-produced until World War I.

Crocheting as well as other handcrafts regained popularity in recent years twenty-first century, thanks to new patterns and the use of vibrant colors.

HOW TO MAKE CROCHET:

It's all about the way we do things. The 'starting chain' is crucial in the creation of crochet fabric. The numbers of stitches are necessary for the first row of fabric as well as the number of chains needed to achieve the right height of the very first stitch in the first row define the length of the beginning chain.

Each stitch can have more than two chains. Each row of crochet is made up of one or more major chains. The hook is then raised to the height of the row's first stitch. The amount of chains utilized for turning is determined by the stitch height.

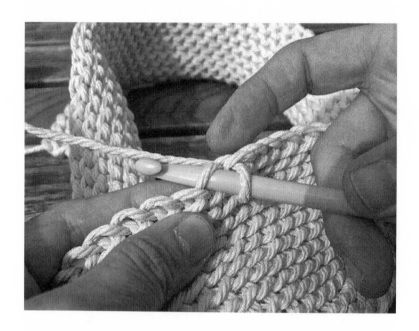

PART 2: STEP-BY-STEP ON HOW TO CROCHET

Before we jump into the various crochet Bralette patterns we have for you, it is essential we explain the various step-by-step approach on how to crochet.

The following are various steps:

STEP 1: CREATE A SLIP KNOT

Place the yarn across as well as a loop it to start the slip knot. Ensure the tail of the small piece is on top of the long yarn and, on to the longer yarn, flip everything over with your thumb as well as forefinger, grab the middle yarn, and slowly take it out. Hold on to the tail and tighten the loop.

STEP 2: TIGHTEN THE LOOP PROCESS

In your left hand, grab the loop as well as slip the hook into it, tightening the loop appropriately around the hook. It shouldn't be too tight; there ought to be some   leeway.

STEP 3: HOLDING OF THREAD

Bend the long part of the yarn of the string through your index finger as well as around your pinkie with your ring fingers, hold the short side at the back in your right hand, then hold the hook. This method of holding the yarn including the hook allows the hook to freely move while maintaining friction on the yarn.

STEP 4: START THE CHAIN PROCESS

Firstly, you can start by tightening the yarn around the hook that you are holding as well as pulling it all the way through the loop for the first chain stitch.

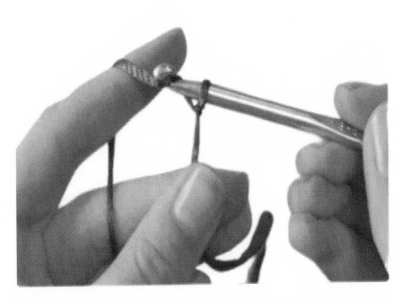

STEP 5: ENSURE YOU FINISH THE CHAIN PROCESS

In this process ensure that the loop is not too tight as well as continue to the next loop by just pulling the yarn through the loop. Continue the process on till you have a chain.

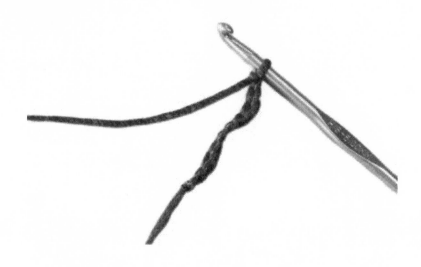

STEP 6: START THE FIRST ROW

Firstly ensure that you place the hooks in the chain directly from the hook so that you can start the process of the first row of the single crochet.

STEP 7: CROCHET THE CHAIN ROW:

With the hook, hold the yarn in your left hand as well as draw it into the first loop. This will provide you two loops that are on your hook, and again through your hook, pick up the yarn as well as pull it into both loops. keep on in this approach until you get to the end of the chained row.

Crochet further rows by chaining one stitch directly at the end of each row and turning the crocheting over to begin the next row.

STEP 8: LAST PROCESS

Finally, ensure that you cut the yarn as well as pull it into the loop to stop

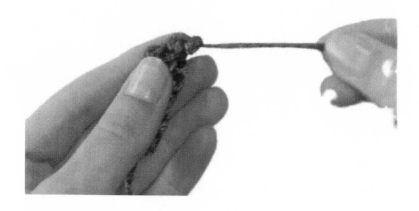

PART 3:CROCHET BRALETTE PATTERNS

Bras may be quite inconvenient and uncomfortable. They can pierce your ribs and cause pain in your back as well as your neck. They may also be your biggest foe when it's warm outside. Instead of wearing a tight and uncomfortable bra, opt for crochet bralette.

WHAT IS A BRALETTE?

A bralette is a bra with no lining as well as no structure. They contain no connections and just little padding. They are not available in standard bra sizes. Instead, they're available in standard sizes like small, medium, and big. A bralette can be worn alone or under beneath clothing.

HOW TO WEAR A CROCHET BRALETTE.

Bralettes aren't the same as regular bras. You are not required to conceal them underneath your shirt. There are several ways to appear stylish while wearing a bralette.

You can wear a bralette with/to:

- Anywhere you want to go mostly beech and other places of relaxations.
- You can wear it with a leather jacket.

- You can wear it with low-back shirts.
- More compactable when you wear it under a loose tee-shirt.
- Wear it under a sheer or lace shirt.

PART 4: YOUR FIRST CROCHET BRALETTE

Start with a crochet Bra cup:

Crocheting bra cups may be a difficult process, everyone's breasts are of various sizes, and it's difficult to cater to all of them in this book but with this process, you will be able to create different bralette patterns. The most difficult aspect of creating a bralette is the   bra   cup.

The summer holiday comes in a slew of halter tops as well as bikinis that necessitate the ability to crochet a bralette.

BASIC THINGS TO PUT IN PLACE WHEN CREATING CROCHETS BRALETTE CUP

The followings are things you need to put into considerations when creating a crochet bra cup.

KNOW THE DIMENSION LEVEL:

You would not want cups that look flat. We need a good shape and dimension, otherwise, we will end up with a side breast, which is not comfortable for many ladies prefer.

BRALETTE CUP WEIGHT AND SIZE:

Although the width of your cup is a personal opinion, you should make sure that it is broad enough to accommodate your breasts adequately. A simple size chart may be found further down on guidelines for sizing your cups.

STITCH TYPE:

Gaps/spaces within stitches in patterns such as the Single Crochet (SC), Double Crochet (DC) as well as Half-Double Crochet (HDC). I always choose the Single Crochet (SC) stitch since it's easy, secure, and gives the wearer confidence.

FIBRE TYPE:

The majority of crocheters who make bra cups use them to make bikini tops as well as halter tops. If that's the situation, the person wearing the top will very likely be in a sweltering setting. Cotton is without a doubt one of the greatest fibers to work with. Mercerized cotton is not the greatest choice in my opinion. I just mention that because I believe that standard cotton yarns, such as Paintbox Yarns Cotton

Aran as well as Paintbox Yarns Cotton DK, are excellent for the completed result and look much nicer. This is entirely a personal choice.

TRIANGLE BRA CUP PATTERN

We are going to create a simple triangle bra pattern that will get you started.

MATERIAL NEEDED:

- You need a 3.50-3.75mm F crochet hook but if you are a tight stitcher you can use 3.50mm.
- You can use any weight of 4-5 yarn. However, preferable paint box yarns cotton aran.
- You will need a tape for your measurement.
- A scissors.

PATTERN NOTES

Sizing preference	This design makes a triangular cup that may be adjusted to fit your needs.
Body shape size	Every woman's body and form is unique. These are suggested sizes; you can change them as required.
Stitch tag	In the third SC of every row's "3 SC," place a stitched tag. This will assist you in determining where you should position your "3 SC" in each row.
Foundation row	Your Foundation Row should be around 3 inches long. For each chain you add and remove to the Foundation Row, you will have to add or delete 2 stitches.

FOUNDATION ROW:

FR	Chain 15 (Three inches approximately)
RW 1	Ensure that the second chain from the hook, SC 13 across, and in the next stitch should be 3 SC.
RW 2 (opposite side)	Turn 29 stitches, Ch 1, and Sc 13
RW 2	Beginning with the first stitch, SC 14 across. Subsequent stitch: <ul><li>3 SC</li><li>14 SC</li><li>CHI 1</li><li>Turn 31 stitches</li></ul>
RW 3	Beginning with the first sts. 15 SC across. Subsequent sts: <ul><li>3 SC</li><li>15 SC</li><li>CH 1</li></ul>

	• Turn 33 sts
RW 4	Beginning with the first sts. 16 SC across. Subsequent sts: 3 SC 16 SC CH 1 Turn 35 sts

Proceed with this pattern on till you get to the size and width of your bra cup.

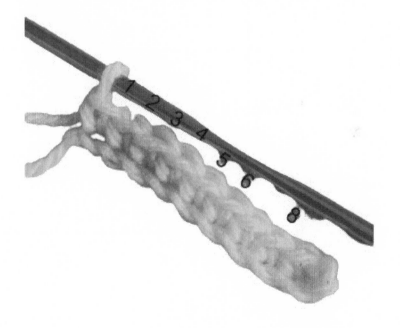

FR	RW1 STS	RW 2 STS	RW 3 STS	RW 4 STS	RW 5 STS	RW 6 STS	RW 7 STS
10	19	21	23	25	27	29	31
11	21	23	25	27	29	31	33
12	23	25	27	29	31	33	35
13	25	27	29	31	33	35	37
14	27	29	31	33	35	37	39
15	29	31	33	35	37	39	41
16	31	33	35	37	39	41	43
17	33	35	37	39	41	43	45
18	35	37	39	41	43	45	47
19	37	39	41	43	45	47	49
20	39	41	43	45	47	49	51

RW *8 STS: 33, 37, 37, 39, 41, 43, 45, 47, 49, 51, and 53

After you are done with cup 1 then follow the same process to make CUP 2.

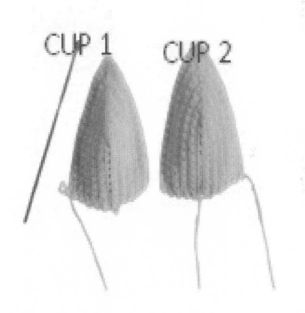

CUP 1 CUP 2

Ensure that you don't blind off after you have created CUP 2.

Place hook through the corner of cup #1 (as seen above) as well as work 1 single crochet using yarn still hooked to cup # 2. (At this point, cups #1 and #2 will be combined.) Keep on working 1 single crochet into each stitch and along the bottom border of cup # 1's bottom edge.

Chain 2 and turn. In the preceding row, work 1 double crochet into each single crochet. Continue crocheting double crochet rows until your bralette reaches the desired length. Remove the ties.

Chain 70 stitches from the top of the bralette cup to the bottom. Bind off and do the same with the other cup. Sew any tails and clip them off.

Hopefully, that wasn't too difficult to comprehend.

PART 5: CROCHET BRALETTE PATTERNS

The projected warmer days will arrive sooner than we anticipated. These Crochet Bralette Styles will assist you to plan ahead of time so you can embrace the summer to the fullest.

I have compiled a list of Crochet Bralettes options for you to get your imagination going. These suggestions are ideal for beach or a stroll through the city. Below are your next adorable and comfortable summer crochet projects you can engage yourself in and be creative on.

TWISTED BRALETTE:

A twisted bralette is one of the best design bralettes you can wear during your summer period. This twisted bralette has a ribbed design beneath the bust as well as connects all the way around to the back, as well as criss-cross straps. This design can be done in different sizes S-M-L depends on your body size.

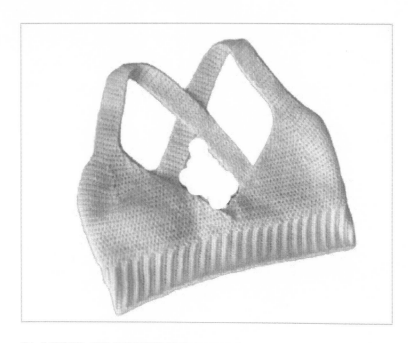

CLASSIC CROCHET BRALETTE:

This crochet bralette design is one of the best you will love to have. a starting point if you want a traditional appearance or just want to relax. The ribbed band, as well as the v-top, are the two main parts.

Don't worry if you have never done ribbing before. It's a lot simpler than you think because this pattern will walk you through the process.

SEABREEZE BRALETTE CROCHET:

This design will bring out your inner hippy. This incredibly cute bralette/crop top is ideal for the summertime. Wear it alone or wearr it with a vest, tank top, or v-neck tee. This is ideal for festivals, holidays, and everyday use. You may use whatever size crochet hook and whichever type of yarn you like.

TIE BACK BRALETTE CROCHET:

This basic bralette adds a unique twist to the blend. In the front, the two cups cross over each other, and the rear is tied with a criss-cross pattern. It's ideal for practicing your bralette cups and is also very beginner-friendly. This bralette is both adorable and easy to create.

COLETTE BRALETTE CROCHET:

This Colette Bralette/Festival Set is ideal for a variety of situations. For a night out on the town, combined with a lovely pair of black jeans and some sneakers. For a more casual approach, wear it with a slouchy sweater and combine it with torn jeans as well as boots. This bralette is both adorable and easy to create.

CLOSED-EDGE BRALETTE CROCHET:

This is a cute small bralette top that may be worn alone or under a button-top or light shirt in the hot summer period. This is a simple and quick craft to make. This pattern is quite simple to follow, and the size is spot on. This bralette is both adorable and easy to create.

SUNRISE BRALETTE CROCHETS:

It's so much fun to make as well as wear. The cups as well as the band are flexible straps, have a lot of detail. You can create three sizes: XS (A cup), S (B cup), M (C cup), as well as L (D+) depend on your size. This bralette is both adorable and easy to create.

EASY CUT BRALETTE CROCHET:

This crochet upper surface offers an alternative approach to a bralette if you do prefer a bit extra free cover. Another wonderful piece for beach days as well as hot summer evenings, it is an amazing bralette that you can create with wonderful layouts like tight stitch across the breast and a little excitement all-around breast region.

EASY-LINKBELL BRALETTE:

This is one of the beautiful bralettes we ever have. It comes with a bra cup attached to an under-tightening cover.

You can wear it to the beach, the pool, a music festival and caught some fun out there, etc.

SIMPLE BRALETTE CROCHET:

This is easy to make mostly for beginners and it is well compactable during the summer period.

You can wear it to the beach, the pool, a music festival and caught some fun out there, etc.

HALTER TOP CROCHET:

The bralette is perfect for people who wish to try something new. It is ideal for strolling in the park or doing grocery shopping.

BRISTOL BRALETTE CROCHET:

This is the ideal bralette design for the summer. It's light as well as breezy, and it will keep you feel cool on hot summer days.

This is a pattern for a more proficient beginner. You can create a bralette of this type in small, moderate, and big sizes. The bralette is sewn together from various pieces. You will need to know how to chain, single crochet, double crochet, and seam.

SHASA BRALETTE VROCHET

The Sasha Crochet Bralette is made entirely of crochet. It has a lace-up back that allows for a little more flexibility in sizing.

This free crochet bralette pattern is designed for intermediate crocheters. You will also need to know how to stitch as well as chain and slip stitch also single crochet, single crochet back loop alone, and half double crochet to finish this design.

SIMPLE BRALETTE CROCHET:

This simple crochet bralette is one of the most beautiful bralettes. It will quickly become your new favorite mostly for going out. The design is simple to follow and may be done by someone new to crocheting.

MEADOW TIE BRALETTE:

This top is ideal for the summer period. You can wear it to the beach, the pool, a music festival and caught some fun out there, etc. This look well with swim trunks, shorts, and perhaps even full-length skirts. Half double crochet BLO (back loop only), single crochet, as well as other fundamental stitches are utilized in these beginner-level crochet designs or patterns.

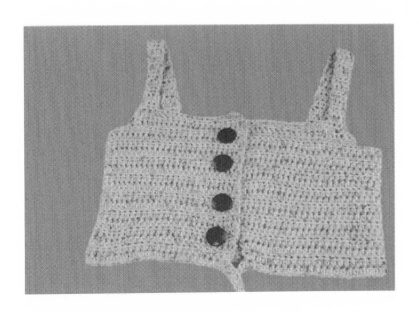

Made in the USA
Middletown, DE
18 June 2023